Understanding Your Faith

A Christian Guide for Spiritual Connection and Growth

E. Dwayne Cantrell

WIPF & STOCK · Eugene, Oregon

Understanding Your Faith
A Christian Guide for Spiritual Connection and Growth

© 2007 by E. Dwayne Cantrell

Wipf and Stock Publishers
199 W 8th Ave, Suite 3
Eugene, OR 97401

Understanding Your Faith
A Christian Guide for Spiritual Connection and Growth
By Cantrell, E. Dwayne
Copyright©2007 by Cantrell, E. Dwayne
ISBN 13: 978-1-55635-722-0
ISBN 10: 1-55635-722-2
Publication date 11/19/2007

Table of Contents

Introduction

There comes a time in our lives when we find ourselves seeking something that will satisfy us. Some people turn to other people to bring satisfaction. They feel that by surrounding themselves with friends, by engaging in intimate dating relationships or even getting married, that fulfillment will take place. While there is nothing wrong with healthy relationships with others, in fact we need them, many people find that there is still something missing.

For others, personal achievement becomes the life pursuit. Whether working toward diplomas, certificates, or licenses, or striving toward earning special titles, positions or awards, people can find themselves on never-ending journeys toward fulfillment. The fact remains that after every title is earned, every dollar is made, and every accolade is achieved, people still find that deep down inside, something is still missing.

Others try to fill the void inside with excessive behavior and actions. By overindulging in food, alcoholic beverages, drugs, shopping, and various other pleasures, people try to find fulfillment in life. Yet many come to the realization that true fulfillment cannot come through these things. In fact, an excess of these types of behaviors can lead to physical deterioration, as well as deepened discontentment.

Understanding Your Faith will begin to address some of the issues we have with fulfillment, or lack thereof, in our lives. It will answer some foundational questions such as, "What are we looking for?" "Who are we looking for?" "What is being offered?" "How do we make the connection?" and "Who's walking with us?"

These questions will be answered from a Christian perspective using Biblical insights.

This teaching is for anyone who is on a spiritual journey who is looking for insights into how to find true fulfillment in life. Though the goal is not to attempt to answer all of life's questions, the content that lies before you will prayerfully shine some light on your path toward spiritual enlightenment.

About this book:

1. Unless otherwise noted, all scriptures contained within are from the New International Version (NIV) of the Holy Bible.

2. Scriptures are listed by the name of the book, followed by the chapter of the book and the specific verse(s). For example, "John 3:16" would mean the book of John, chapter 3, verse 16.

3. At the end of each session you will find a section titled, "Notes/Personal Reflection." You may use this section to list questions, to note aspects of the session that speak to you in a special way or to simply journal your personal thoughts about your spiritual walk. You are also encouraged to take notes throughout this book on any page you choose. This should be a "working" book as you process your faith and understanding.

SESSION 1: WHAT ARE WE LOOKING FOR?
Understanding our Spiritual Journey

Creation:

Without debating creation and evolution, let's begin with the premise stated in the Bible that we were created in the image of God.

"So God created man in his own image, in the image of God he created him; male and female he created them."
Genesis 1:27

If we were created in the image of God, then we know that we were created with a spirit.

"God is spirit, and his worshipers must worship in spirit and in truth."   *John 4:24*

Connection:

From the moment of birth, we are on a journey to find a spiritual connection.

Have you ever asked the following questions?

- What is the purpose of life?
- Why was I born?
- Is this as good as it gets?
- Is there something else I should be doing?

Have you ever made the following statements?

- I've had many things, but nothing seems to satisfy me
- I know there is something else out there
- It seems like something is missing in my life

Do any of these bumper-sticker statements sound familiar?[1]

- ✆ "Life <stinks>…and then you die"
- ✆ "He who dies with the most toys wins"
- ✆ "Reality is the only obstacle to happiness"
- ✆ "My life has a superb cast but I can't figure out the plot"

As we experience daily routines and cycles of life we come to two realizations:

The first is, *"What has been will be again, what has been done will be done again; there is nothing new under the sun."*
Ecclesiastes 1:9

Second, no matter how many physical activities we involve ourselves in, how many physical achievements we accomplish, or how many physical things we surround ourselves with, until we establish a spiritual connection to God we will never truly be fulfilled.

Confusion:

This spiritual journey that we embark upon can be very confusing. Because it is a spiritual journey, the process toward enlightenment may not be logical.

Because we are both physical beings and spiritual beings, just as physical fulfillment will not satisfy us spiritually, spiritual fulfillment may not satisfy us physically. Therefore there will, at times, exist an inner conflict between your body and your spirit.

Another confusing aspect of the spiritual journey is that there are so many philosophies and religions that seem to say the same thing. Let's look at some examples[2] of how different belief systems have similarities.

✍ *"Be content with what you have; rejoice in the way things are. When you realize there is nothing lacking, the whole world belongs to you."*

Lao Tzu, Chinese Philosopher/founder of Taoism

✍ *"He who is not contented with what he has, would not be contented with what he would like to have"*

Socrates

✍ *"He who desires happiness must strive after a perfectly contented disposition and control himself, for happiness has contentment for its root, the root of unhappiness is the contrary disposition."*

Guru Nanak, Indian Spiritual Leader

✍ *"I know what it is to be in need, and I know what it is to have plenty. I have learned the secret of being **content** in any and every situation, whether well fed or hungry, whether living in plenty or in want."*

Philippians 4:12

Questions:

1. Can you remember a time in your life when it seemed like something was missing? What were some of the things you did to try to bring fulfillment to your life? (ie. a new job, a new look, moving to a new location, a new relationship, etc.) Did it/they work?

    _____
    _____
    _____
    _____
    _____

2. Have you ever wondered which religion or philosophy
    was the right one? As mentioned earlier in this chapter,
    many seem to say the right things. What are some of the
    experiences or questions that you have had about various
    religions?

    _____

    _____

    _____

    _____

    _____

3. According to the previous chapter, can all religions lead
    to the same God? Why or why not?

    _____

    _____

    _____

    _____

Conclusion:

Spiritual matters are confusing in a physical world. That is why
throughout history, people have sought the wisdom of
philosophers, teachers, and spiritual leaders for insight and
direction. While the philosophies and teachings from many
perspectives bear truth, as represented on the previous page, we
believe that the only way to achieve the ultimate state of being is
through a connection to your creator, who is God.

We also believe that Jesus is our only connection to God:

*"For God did not send his Son into the world to condemn the
world, but to save the world through him."*
John 3:17

"Jesus answered, 'I am the way and the truth and the life. No one comes to the Father except through me.'"
                    John 14:6

"For God so loved the world that he gave his one and only Son, that whoever believes in him shall not perish but have eternal life."   *John 3:16*

Though this process may be frustrating at times, don't give up on your journey. Your purpose, your destiny, your contribution to this world and your eternity are all at hand through your spiritual pursuit.

PERSONAL THOUGHTS AND REFLECTIONS

_____

_____

_____

_____

_____

_____

_____

_____

_____

_____

_____

_____

_____

_____

_____

SESSION 2: WHO ARE WE LOOKING FOR?
Understanding God

As mentioned in Session 1, we believe that on the road of our spiritual journey we find ourselves pursuing a connection to our creator, God. In this session, we will seek a greater understanding of God, and His attributes in an effort to discover the relationship between God and our life's purpose.

The goal of this session is to understand the three major aspects (or persons) of God and what meaning they bear in our lives.

To approach an examination of God we have to understand three things. First, we must understand that God <u>Is</u>.

"God said to Moses, 'I am who I am . This is what you are to say to the Israelites: 'I AM has sent me to you.' God also said to Moses, 'Say to the Israelites, 'The LORD, the God of your fathers—the God of Abraham, the God of Isaac and the God of Jacob—has sent me to you.' This is my name forever, the name by which I am to be remembered from generation to generation."
Exodus 3:14-15

Second, we must understand what God is not.

"God is not a man, that he should lie, nor a son of man, that he should change his mind. Does he speak and then not act? Does he promise and not fulfill?"
Numbers 23:19

Third it important to know what God is.

"God is spirit, and his worshipers must worship in spirit and in truth."   *John 4:24*

As we look to understand God, we often use what are referred to as "anthro-po-morph-isms" to describe God in terms that we can understand. An anthropomorphism is a human term given to something that is not human.[3]

Fundamental Thoughts:

✍ God is beyond definition – Attempting to define God is like attempting to count the number of grains of sand on a beach.

✍ Many aspects of God will always remain a mystery. Because we are human beings, many matters in the spiritual realm will remain mysteries to us.

✍ If everything could be defined and understood, it would no longer be faith…it would be science. God's desire is not to hide things from us, but the wonders of God are incomprehensible to us. For example, we may never understand the depth of God's love for us.

Attributes of God (The Father):

As we pursue identification with God, we will also view the attributes of Jesus and the Holy Spirit. The reason for viewing God, Jesus and the Holy Spirit will be explained later in this chapter.

Listed below are some of the attributes of God. The purpose of ascribing attributes to God is not so we can define God, for that is impossible, but so that we can have identification to, and an understanding of our relationship with God.

The definition of attribute is, "an inherent characteristic."[4] Listed below are just some of the many attributes of God.

1. God is supreme in power in position to all others. Nothing is out of God's control. This is called sovereignty.

2. God is unchanging in nature and character. This is referred to as immutability.

3. There was never a time that God did not exist. God has no beginning and no end. This means that God is eternal.

4. God is all knowing or omniscient.

5. God is all powerful or omnipotent.

6. God is everywhere at the same time which is also known as omnipresent.

7. God is "separate" from sin and evil. This is the primary definition of holy.

8. God is morally correct and sets the moral standard. This means that God is righteous.

9. God shows fairness in everything that he does. This speaks of God's justice.

10. It is impossible for God to lie. Therefore, God is truth.

11. God is benevolent and good. God is loving toward, and desires love from his creation. God is love.

12. God shows compassion for those who oppose his will. God is merciful.

Attributes of Jesus (The Son):

Below you will find some of the many attributes of Jesus. You will notice that some attributes are similar, and some are different than those of God. The reason for these similarities and differences will be explained later.

1.   The Word of God/God:

> *"In the beginning was the Word, and the Word was with God, and the Word was God. He was with God in the beginning."   John 1:1-2*

> *"The Word became flesh and made his dwelling among us. We have seen his glory, the glory of the One and Only, who came from the Father, full of grace and truth."*
> *John 1:14*

2.   Sovereign:

> *"Therefore God exalted him to the highest place and gave him the name that is above every name, that at the name of Jesus every knee should bow, in heaven and on earth and under the earth, and every tongue confess that Jesus Christ is Lord, to the glory of God the Father."*
> *Philippians 2:9-11*

3.   Eternal:

> *"Behold, I am coming soon! My reward is with me, and I will give to everyone according to what he has done. I am the Alpha and the Omega, the First and the Last, the Beginning and the End."*
> *Revelation 2:12-13*

4.   "Only begotten" Son:

"For God so loved the world that he gave his one and only Son, that whoever believes in him shall not perish but have eternal life."
John 3:16

5.   Forgiver of sins:

"Now some teachers of the law were sitting there, thinking to themselves, 'Why does this fellow talk like that? He's blaspheming! Who can forgive sins but God alone?'"   Mark 2:6-7

Jesus responded, "But that you may know that the Son of Man has authority on earth to forgive sins . . . ."
Mark 2:10

Attributes of the Holy Spirit:

"And I will ask the Father, and <u>he will give</u> you another <u>Counselor</u> to be with you forever— the Spirit of truth. The world cannot accept <u>him</u>, because <u>it neither sees him nor knows him</u>. But you know him, for he lives with you and will be in you."
John 14:16-17

1.   The scriptures refer to the Holy Spirit as a <u>person</u> (notice the word "him")

2.   The Holy Spirit is a <u>counselor</u>

The word for "counselor" is a word that means "called alongside" "helper" "mediator" or "intercessor."[5]

3.   Not seen or known by the world

4.   Sent by God

5.　　Teacher:

"But the Counselor, the Holy Spirit, whom the Father will send in my name, will teach you all things and will remind you of everything I have said to you."
John 14:26

6.　　Truth:

"When the Counselor comes, whom I will send to you from the Father, the Spirit of truth who goes out from the Father, he will testify about me."
John 15:26

7.　　Convictor:

"When he comes, he will convict the world of guilt in regard to sin and righteousness and judgment"
John 16:8

8.　　Guide:

"But when he, the Spirit of truth, comes, he will guide you into all truth. He will not speak on his own; he will speak only what he hears, and he will tell you what is yet to come."　　*John 16:13*

9.　　The Lord is the Spirit

"Now the Lord is the Spirit, and where the Spirit of the Lord is, there is freedom. And we, who with unveiled faces all reflect the Lord's glory, are being transformed into his likeness with ever-increasing glory, which comes from the Lord, who is the Spirit."
2 Corinthians 3:17-18

Explanation:

When pursuing an understanding of God, it is important to learn the persons of God. Though there are many attributes to describe God, there are actually three persons of God that are prevalent throughout the scriptures. These persons are The Father, The Son, and The Holy Spirit.

This concept is known as the Trinity which means *three*. Though this term is not found in scripture, the three persons of God can be found individually and collectively throughout the Bible. Trinity does not mean that there are three Gods. The Trinity is a description of one God existing in three "persons."

For example, each "person" has unique attributes. However, there is one attribute that is common to all.

✺   God is God (we will presume that this needs no explanation)

✺   God is Jesus:

>   *"In the beginning was the Word, and the Word was with God, and the Word was God. He was with God in the beginning."   John 1:1-2*

>   *"The Word became flesh and made his dwelling among us. We have seen his glory, the glory of the One and Only, who came from the Father, full of grace and truth."*
>   *John 1:14*

✺   God is The Holy Spirit:

>   *"Now the Lord is the Spirit, and where the Spirit of the Lord is, there is freedom. And we, who with unveiled faces all reflect the Lord's glory, are being transformed into his likeness with ever-increasing glory, which comes from the Lord, who is the Spirit."*
>   *2 Corinthians 3:17-18*

This is one of the mysteries of God, and is impossible to fully understand. In fact, the greatest scholars and theologians have attempted to define the Trinity and have been criticized for falling short of an adequate description. Again, instead of attempting to define God, it is more important to gain a basic understanding of who God is and how we can relate to God.

Questions:

In this chapter there were a number of attributes mentioned to describe God, Jesus and the Holy Spirit.

1.   Of the attributes mentioned, which ones have you experienced, or believed to be true about:

God   _____
               _____
               _____

Jesus   _____
               _____
               _____

The Holy Spirit _____
               _____
               _____

2.   Which attributes have you <u>not</u> experienced, or find it difficult to believe about:

God   _____
               _____
               _____

Jesus   _____
               _____
               _____

The Holy Spirit _____

_____

_____

Conclusion:

It should encourage us to know that our creator, consisting of three persons, with such a broad range of attributes is our spiritual connection. We have access to the power, protection and peace of God. However, before we can fully experience and appreciate this power we must understand the next step. In Session 3 we will seek to understand salvation. When we have an understanding of salvation, these attributes will:

1.   Be the foundation on which you stand

2.   Be experienced throughout your walk with God

3.   Be revisited regularly, and personalized to
       strengthen your walk

4.   Be a reminder of who God is, and who you are
       in Him through Christ

NOTES/PERSONAL REFLECTION

_____

_____

_____

_____

_____

_____

_____

_____

_____

_____

_____

_____

_____

_____

_____

_____

SESSION 3: WHAT IS BEING OFFERED?
Understanding Salvation

Introduction:

In Session 2, we discussed God and His attributes in an effort to discover the relationship between God and our lives. In this session, we will pursue an understanding of the power of salvation. When we understand the concept and purposes of salvation, we come to a deeper appreciation for the love that God has for us. The goal of this session is to appreciate God's love, so that we can receive His love, and in turn share His love with others. In doing this, we move even closer to discovering our purpose.

Insight:

Sin

Q: What is sin?

A: In general, sin is departure from human or divine standards.[6]

> *"Everyone who sins breaks the law; in fact, sin is lawlessness."*
> *1 John 3:4*

Q: Who sins?

A: Everyone

> *"...for all have sinned and fall short of the glory of God."*
> *Romans 3:23*

> *"If we claim to be without sin, we deceive ourselves and the truth is not in us"*
> *1 John 1:8*

Q: What are the affects of sin?

A.   *"For the wages of sin is death, but the gift of God is eternal life in Christ Jesus our Lord."*
                                    Romans 6:23

      "He will punish those who do not know God and do not obey the gospel of our Lord Jesus. They will be punished with everlasting destruction and shut out from the presence of the Lord and from the majesty of his power."
                                    2 Thessalonians 1:8-10

It is important to note that the word, "death" has different connotations. In one sense, for an individual who has accepted Christ, death can result in loss of hope, faith, esteem, self worth, etc. Yet in another sense, death refers to the eternal punishment that one receives without accepting Christ and the forgiveness he offers through Salvation.

Salvation

Q: What is salvation? / What are you saved from?

A.   It is being saved from the power and dominion of sin in our life, and from an eternity separated from God.

Q: How are we saved?

A.   There are three simple phases to receiving salvation from God:

Phase 1: Believe in who Jesus is:

"For God so loved the world that he gave his <u>one and only Son</u>, that whoever believes in him shall not perish but have eternal life."   *John 3:16*

24

"In the beginning was the Word, and the Word was with God, and the Word was God. He was with God in the beginning."
John 1:1-2

"The Word became flesh and made his dwelling among us. We have seen his glory, the glory of the One and Only, who came from the Father, full of grace and truth."
John 1:14

"...while we wait for the blessed hope—the glorious appearing of our great God and Savior, Jesus Christ, who gave himself for us to redeem us from all wickedness and to purify for himself a people that are his very own, eager to do what is good"
Titus 2:13

Phase 2: Believe in what Jesus did:

"For what I received I passed on to you as of first importance: that Christ died for our sins according to the Scriptures, that he was buried, that he was raised on the third day according to the Scriptures, and that he appeared to Peter, and then to the Twelve. After that, he appeared to more than five hundred of the brothers at the same time, most of whom are still living, though some have fallen asleep. Then he appeared to James, then to all the apostles, and last of all he appeared to me also, as to one abnormally born."
1 Corinthians 15:3-8

Phase 3: Confess your belief

"That if you confess with your mouth, 'Jesus is Lord.' and believe in your heart that God raised him from the dead, you will be saved. For it is with your heart that you believe and are justified, and it is with your mouth that you confess and are saved." *Romans 10:9-10*

If you believe in the above, you are a Christian!

Q.   How can I be sure that I'm saved?

A.   There are many ways that a person experiences and
        displays evidence of salvation. Three of them are:

☙   The Spirit's work in us produces change in you

*"Therefore, if anyone is in Christ, he is a new creation; the old
has gone, the new has come!"*
                                2 Corinthians 5:17

☙   You desire to follow God's teachings

*"Jesus replied, 'If anyone loves me, he will   obey my teaching.
My Father will love him, and we will come to him and make our
home with him. He who does not love me will not obey my
teaching. These words you hear are not my own; they belong to
the Father who sent me.'"*
                                John 14:23-24

*"We know that we have come to know him if we obey his
commands. The man who says, 'I know him,' but does not do
what he commands is a liar, and the truth is not in him. But if
anyone obeys his word, God's love is truly made complete in him.
This is how we know we are in him"*
                                1 John 2:3-4

☙   The Spirit of God dwells in you

*"And this is his command: to believe in the name of his Son,
Jesus Christ, and to love one another as he commanded us. Those
who obey his commands live in him, and he in them. And this is
how we know that he lives in us: We know it by the Spirit he gave
us."*   *1 John 3:23-24*

Questions:

1.   If I died today, where would I go?

_____

_____

_____

2.   I believe this because…

_____

_____

_____

3.   If I want to receive salvation, or if I would like to offer
      God's gift of salvation to someone else, what are the
      "phases"?

- _____
- _____
- _____

Conclusion:

God wants you to know that through faith you have eternal life.
It is not His will that we live our lives wondering daily if we are
saved. If at times you are unsure of your salvation remember that
our salvation rests only on God's finished work for us through
Christ.

*"For it is by grace you have been saved, through faith—and this
not from yourselves, it is the gift of God—not by works, so that no
one can boast. For we are God's workmanship, created in Christ
Jesus to do good works, which God prepared in advance for us to
do."*

Ephesians 2:8-10

NOTES/PERSONAL REFLECTION

_____

_____

_____

_____

_____

_____

_____

_____

_____

_____

_____

_____

_____

_____

_____

_____

SESSION 4: HOW DO WE MAKE THE CONNECTION?
Understanding Prayer

Introduction:

In Session 3, we developed an understanding of the concept and purposes of salvation, and we, prayerfully, came to a deeper appreciation for the love that God has for us. In Session 2, we learned that we can enhance our relationship with God though learning about His attributes.

However, we can further strengthen our relationship with God through the process of communication. Communication consists of both verbal and non-verbal expression between individuals. In this session, we will learn how to communicate with God through prayer.

Insight:

The best way to get to know someone is to talk with that person often. God longs for you to know Him. The Bible is full of invitations to enter into a deep, personal relationship with God.

"And you, my son Solomon, acknowledge the God of your father, and serve him with wholehearted devotion and with a willing mind, for the LORD searches every heart and understands every motive behind the thoughts. If you seek him, he will be found by you; but if you forsake him, he will reject you forever."
1 Chronicles 28:9

"I love those who love me, and those who seek me find me."
Proverbs 8:17

Q: What is prayer?

A: Prayer is simply conversation with God. The concept of carrying on a conversation with an invisible being that does not respond audibly might seem foolish. But we can recall from Session 1 what the Bible states about God:

> *"God is spirit, and his worshipers must worship in spirit and in truth."*
> *John 4:24*

This is one of the areas where our reason and our faith will have a tendency to compete with each other. The mind might lead us to believe that prayer is an empty and meaningless process, while our spirit will desire conversation with, and connection to God.

Q: Where should we pray?

A: There are two examples that we get from the Bible:

✍   We should pray alone

"But when you pray, go into your room, close the door and pray to your Father, who is unseen. Then your Father, who sees what is done in secret, will reward you."
Matthew 6:6-7

"Very early in the morning, while it was still dark, Jesus got up, left the house and went off to a <u>solitary place</u>, where he prayed."
Mark 1:35

"Yet the news about him spread all the more, so that crowds of people came to hear him and to be healed of their sicknesses. But Jesus often withdrew to lonely places and prayed."
Luke 5:15-16

✍   We should pray with others

"They all joined together constantly in prayer, along with the women and Mary the mother of Jesus, and with his brothers."
                    Acts 1:14

"When they heard this, they raised their voices together in prayer to God..."
                    Acts 4:24

Q: When should we pray?

A: There are three times/occasions that we should pray:

✍   Early

        "<u>Very early</u> in the morning, while it was still dark, Jesus got up, left the house and went off to a solitary place, where he prayed."
                    Mark 1:35

✍   Always

        "Then Jesus told his disciples a parable to show them that they should always pray and not give up."
                    Luke 18:1

✍   Continually

        "Be joyful always; pray continually; give thanks in all circumstances, for this is God's will for you in Christ Jesus."
                    1 Thessalonians 5:16-18

Q: Why should we pray?

A: There are many reasons why we should pray. Here are
       three that we find in scripture:

✆   To have a closer relationship with God:

*"The LORD is <u>near</u> to all who call on him, to all who call on him
in truth."*
                                        Psalm 145:18

✆   For strength against temptation:

*"Jesus went out as usual to the Mount of Olives, and his disciples
followed him. On reaching the place, he said to them, 'Pray that
you will not fall into temptation.'"*
                                        Luke 22:39-40

✆   For the strength of fellow Christians as so eloquently
       exemplified in the text below:

*"For this reason I kneel before the Father, from whom his whole
family in heaven and on earth derives its name. I pray that out of
his glorious riches he may strengthen you with power through his
Spirit in your inner being, so that Christ may dwell in your hearts
through faith. And I pray that you, being rooted and established
in love, may have power, together with all the saints, to grasp
how wide and long and high and deep is the love of Christ, and to
know this love that surpasses knowledge—that you may be filled
to the measure of all the fullness of God."*
                                        Ephesians 3:14-20

Q: How does prayer work?

A: Prayer works by the Holy Spirit acting on our behalf. In
       the same way that we pray on behalf of our families,
       friends and people around the world, the Holy Spirit prays
       for us. This is called intercession or interceding. The

difference is that the Holy Spirit actually interprets our hearts for us in ways we cannot express in words. We find this in the following passage:

"In the same way, the Spirit helps us in our weakness. We do not know what we ought to pray for, but the Spirit himself intercedes for us with groans that words cannot express. And he who searches our hearts knows the mind of the Spirit, because the Spirit intercedes for the saints in accordance with God's will."
Romans 8:26-27

In Session 2 we learned that two of God's attributes are love and mercy (or compassion). These attributes help us to embrace the fact that God not only gives believers the Holy Spirit to interpret the expressions of our hearts, but God even understands our tears.

"Even now my witness is in heaven; my advocate is on high. My intercessor is my friend as my eyes pour out tears to God; on behalf of a man he pleads with God as a man pleads for his friend."
Job 16:19-21

Q: How should we pray?

A: There are two important things to remember as we pray:

☙   Be yourself!

"And when you pray, do not keep on babbling like pagans, for they think they will be heard because of their many words. Do not be like them, for your Father knows what you need before you ask him."
Matthew 6:7-8

✍   Be confident!

"This is the confidence we have in approaching God: that if we ask anything according to his will, he hears us."
                                    1 John 5:14

As we learn tangible steps for prayer, let's look first at how Jesus replied when asked, "How should we pray?"

"This, then, is how you should pray: 'Our Father in heaven, hallowed be your name, your kingdom come, your will be done on earth as it is in heaven. Give us today our daily bread. Forgive us our debts, as we also have forgiven our debtors. And lead us not into temptation, but deliver us from the evil one.'"
                                    Matthew 6:9-13

This next lesson will give us a step-by-step guide which will help us as we pray. This teaching is entitled,

The A.R.T. of Prayer

We can view prayer as an art form which we express, in our own way, our hearts to God. This piece of art, if you will, looks and sounds different from one person to another and is a reflection of who we are.

Though the words of our prayers may be similar, the hearts from which the prayers originate can be vastly different. However, as a model that reflects Jesus' answer to the question, "How should we pray?" the following acrostic may be helpful:

A =   Acknowledge
R =   Request
T =   Thank

✐ Acknowledge

When we call someone whom we love and respect on the telephone, the first thing we usually say is, "Hello." This is our way of acknowledging that person as we begin our conversation.

In the same way, as we approach a conversation with God, we want to appropriately acknowledge Him to remind us of three important things:

1. Who we are talking to?

"I will exalt you, my God the King; I will praise your name for ever and ever. Every day I will praise you and extol your name for ever and ever. Great is the LORD and most worthy of praise; his greatness no one can fathom."
Psalm 145:1-3

2. God is all-powerful (remember Session 2)

"Now to him who is able to do immeasurably more than all we ask or imagine, according to his power that is at work within us"
Ephesians 3:20

3. He is our Father and we are His children

"How great is the love the Father has lavished on us, that we should be called children of God!"
1 John 3:1

✐ Request

When we make our requests known to God, there are a number of areas that could, and should be addressed. However, before we simply begin asking for God to give us things, we need to be mindful of our relationships with God and others.

For example, when I was a child there was a time that I was playing in the house, which was against my mother's rules, and I broke a window. When my mother came home from work and noticed the broken window, of course she wanted to know what happened. When I told her that I broke the window as a result of playing in the house, she was angry.

Now, if at that moment I were to ask my mother for a new bike, I can only imagine what her response might have been. First, asking my mother for something after I just violated her rules would be highly insensitive to her, and to our relationship. Asking my mother to give me something in these circumstances would have been incredibly selfish and it would be no surprise if the answer, if one was given at all, was no.

Likewise, there are areas that we must be mindful of when we begin to ask God to give us something or to do something for us. Below is an example of five step-by-step requests that we should ask of God when we pray:

1.   Forgiveness for our sins (be specific)

"If we confess our sins, he is faithful and just and will forgive us our sins and purify us from all unrighteousness."
                    1 John 1:9

2.   Forgiveness of those who have sinned against you

"And when you stand praying, if you hold anything against anyone, forgive him, so that your Father in heaven may forgive you your sins."   *Mark 11:25*

3.   God's provision for your needs

"Ask and it will be given to you; seek and you will find; knock and the door will be opened to you. For everyone who asks receives; he who seeks finds; and to him who knocks, the door will be opened"   *Matt 7:7-8*

When asking God to provide for our needs we need to ask ourselves the following questions:

What's my motive?

"When you ask, you do not receive, because you ask with wrong motives, that you may spend what you get on your pleasures."
James 4:3

Is my request in line with God's will?

"Do not conform any longer to the pattern of this world, but be transformed by the renewing of your mind. Then you will be able to test and approve what God's will is—his good, pleasing and perfect will."
Romans 12:2

Do I have faith?

"The apostles said to the Lord, "Increase our faith!" He replied, "If you have faith as small as a mustard seed, you can say to this mulberry tree, 'Be uprooted and planted in the sea,' and it will obey you."
Luke 17:5-6

4.   God's provision for others

"Therefore confess your sins to each other and pray for each other so that you may be healed."
James 5:16

"And pray in the Spirit on all occasions with all kinds of prayers and requests. With this in mind, be alert and always keep on praying for all the saints."
Ephesians 5:18

5.   That above all else, that God's will would be done

Jesus' words in prayer:

"Going a little farther, he fell with his face to the ground and prayed, "My Father, if it is possible, may this cup be taken from me. Yet not as I will, but as you will."
                                        Matthew 26:39

Jesus' words to us:

"But seek first his kingdom and his righteousness, and all these things will be given to you as well."
                                        Matthew 6:33

✆   Thank

One of the most important elements of our communication with God is being thankful. In fact, as we live life in general, we need to be in a constant state of thankfulness. Having an attitude of thanksgiving toward God will positively impact our disposition as we stand before God in prayer, our appreciation for who God is to us, and our hope for ourselves and others.

There are many things to be thankful for and in our daily communication with God we should express our appreciation constantly, specifically naming those things. Here are five areas in which we can daily thank God:

1.   For all that we already have

2.   For all that He has already done

3.   For hearing our prayers

4.   For answering our prayers both past and future

5.   For salvation through Christ which gave us relationship and access to Him

"Be joyful always; pray continually; give thanks in all circumstances, for this is God's will for you in Christ Jesus."
1 Thessalonians 5:16-18

Questions:

1.   In your own words, what is prayer?

_____
_____
_____

2.   Why is prayer important?

_____
_____
_____

3.   What is the A.R.T. or prayer?

• _____
• _____
• _____

Conclusion:

There is a wonderful song that speaks so well to the relationship that God desires with us. The lyrics of the chorus should motivate us to go to God in prayer. The song says:

"He knows my name…He knows my every thought…He sees each tear that falls…and hears me when I call."[7]

Just as healthy communication is essential to a healthy human relationship, prayer is essential to a healthy relationship with God.

When we **acknowledge** God, it reminds us of the awesome God that we serve, who loves us as children by providing, protecting and guiding us into our destiny.

When we **request** forgiveness from God, we rid ourselves of the negative affects of sin. Through the request of supplication for ourselves and others, we are reminded that God is the source of all of our needs, and that we have the privilege to go to God with our requests.

When we give **thanks** to God, it reminds us that all good things that we have is a result of the grace of God, and humbles us by keeping us from taking our blessings for granted.

In light of the prayer process, we come to the realization that our Christian walk is not meaningful in isolation. As we will learn in the next session, we may be able to pray to God in isolation, but unless we pray with and walk with others, our walk is incomplete.

NOTES/PERSONAL REFLECTION

NOTES/PERSONAL REFLECTION

SESSION 5: WHO'S WALKING WITH US?
Understanding The Church

<u>Introduction:</u>

Have you ever taken a leisurely walk or a hike? If you've ever been on a walk by yourself, you might have experienced great peace. You can reflect, enjoy the weather, take in the scenery, and simply think and breathe. No telephones ringing, babies crying, or projects to complete, just you and the outdoors. Doesn't that sound great? Now what if you're on this wonderful walk and you encounter a vicious animal or simply get lost? While it would be possible to eventually make it through either of these encounters on your own, it would be much better if there were someone else to help you.

This is similar to our spiritual walk. As we discussed in Session 4, there are times when we need to be alone with God. We need to get away from the ringing phones and the responsibilities and nurture our spirit. However, there are also times when we encounter challenges, danger or stray from our path. In these situations we need assistance, guidance and encouragement from others. We also need to assist, guide and encourage others with their walk. In essence, we are all walking together and we all need each other.

<u>"A" Church vs. "The" Church</u>

There is a difference between being a member of <u>a church</u>, and being a member of <u>The Church</u>.

There are different translations of the biblical word used for "church."

1.   One definition of a church is a place where the
      people of God gather. This can also be called an
      assembly or congregation.[8]

"Both the one who makes men holy and those who are made holy are of the same family. So Jesus is not ashamed to call them brothers. He says, 'I will declare your name to my brothers; in the presence of the <u>congregation</u> I will sing your praises.'"
Hebrews 2:11-12

2.   Another definition refers to the <u>global</u> community
        of Christians or the <u>universal</u> church.[9]

"Then <u>the church</u> throughout Judea, Galilee and Samaria enjoyed a time of peace. It was strengthened; and encouraged by the Holy Spirit, it grew in numbers, living in the fear of the Lord."   *Acts 9:31*

Salvation alone makes us members of The Church, or the global community of Christians. However, we must also commit to being members of a church, or local assembly, where we can be active family members as we navigate through our spiritual journey. Once again, this is an area where without both, our spiritual lives are incomplete. This is why Jesus commands us to love God, and love our neighbors.

<u>Support</u>

"A new command I give you: Love one another. As I have loved you, so you must love one another. By this all men will know that you are my disciples, if you love one another."
John 13:14-35

The Bible instructs us to love our neighbor. In fact, we are instructed to love our enemies as well. However, in this particular text, we are instructed to "love one another" as Christians. Our love, encouragement, instruction, support and care for one another shows non-Christians that we are a people who follow Christ.

This type of love in the Christian community gives the world an example of how love should look. If we truly exhibit the love of Christ, then the world around us will have living examples of healthy communities, healthy relationships, and healthy families.

Accountability: Judging vs. Correction
In our society today, we hear phrases like, "You can't judge me," and, "Only God can judge me." While these are true in a sense, the context of the word "judge" needs to be clarified.

1.   One sense of the word judge has to do with condemnation, or pronouncing a sentence or penalty as a ruler, or a judge in a courtroom[10]

2.   Another sense of the word "judge" has to do with forming an opinion based on evidence obtained through observation.[11]

People have no right to condemn or pronounce any sentence on anyone. We are not the ones who determine who goes to hell, or what specific consequences one might receive for a particular sin committed. This is what the Bible refers to as judging, and we are constantly discouraged against this practice.

"Do not judge, or you too will be judged. For in the same   way you judge others, you will be judged, and with the   measure you use, it will be measured to you."
Matthew 7:1-2

"You, then, why do you judge your brother? Or why do you look down on your brother? For we will all stand before God's judgment seat. It is written: 'As surely as I live,' says the Lord, 'every knee will bow before me; every tongue will confess to God.' So then, each of us will give an account of himself to God. Therefore let us stop   passing judgment on one another. Instead, make up your   mind not to put any stumbling block or obstacle in your brother's way."
Romans 14:10-13

"As for the person who hears my words but does not keep them, I do not judge him. For I did not come to judge the world, but to save it."
John 12:47 (The words of Jesus)

However, the Bible does give us standards to live by. As Christians, we are responsible for living the word of God. If we look at the second definition of judge, the word of God speaks clearly about his followers "weighing evidence" and "testing" of each other so that we would be accountable for living what we profess (or practicing what we preach).

Notice what the following scriptures say about standards and testing:

Standards of Living:

"Do not merely listen to the word, and so deceive yourselves. Do what it says."   *James 1:22*

"As the body without the spirit is dead, so faith without deeds is dead."   *James 2:26*

"If you love me, you will obey what I command."
John 14:15

Testing Each Other:

"Watch out for false prophets. They come to you in sheep's clothing, but inwardly they are ferocious wolves. By their fruit you will recognize them."
Matthew 7:15-16a

"Let the word of Christ dwell in you richly as you teach and admonish one another with all wisdom, and as you sing psalms, hymns and spiritual songs with gratitude in your hearts to God."
Colossians 3:16

"I myself am convinced, my brothers, that you yourselves are full of goodness, complete in knowledge and competent to instruct one another."   *Romans 15:14*

"Now we ask you, brothers, to respect those who work hard among you, who are over you in the Lord and who admonish you."   *1 Thessalonians 5:12*

Questions:

1.   What is the difference between "A" church and "The" Church?

_____

_____

_____

2.   What is the difference between judging and testing?

_____

_____

_____

3.   Why should Christians go to church?

_____

_____

_____

Conclusion:

A church is a singular representation of The Church which is the Body of Christ at-large. As Christians, it is important that we join a Body of Believers to support each other, pray for one another, serve each other and serve our local communities. This is how we emulate the works of Jesus. One very important aspect of supporting each other, is lovingly holding each other accountable to our faith. In scriptural context, the word "admonish" in the above verses means to counsel about avoidance of improper conduct, to warn or to instruct.[12] We are not only responsible for living out our faith on our own, but as a community we are to encourage, instruct and even correct one another so that we can all do our best together. As difficult as it is sometimes, Christians need to uphold the honor of the name of the Lord through integrity in how we live. This is best done in a community which is known as The Church.

NOTES/PERSONAL REFLECTION

NOTES/PERSONAL REFLECTION

SESSION 6: WHERE DO WE GO FROM HERE?
Understanding our Walk

Introduction:

As Christians, it is important for us to know how to navigate
through life. Is there a certain way that we are to live on a daily
basis? The answer is yes. The Bible gives us instructions on
how to live holy, fruitful, effective lives.

Many people have a misunderstanding of the word, "holy".
Some believe that holy means to be perfect. The problem with
that is that when we realize that we are not perfect then the
concept of holiness becomes so out of reach that we don't even
want to try.

Another misunderstanding of the word "holy" is the concept of
someone being better than someone else. The term "holier than
thou" comes to mind here. The problem here is that though one
person may have more money, may be more skilled in a
particular area, or may be higher position on the occupational or
social ladder, no person is better than another. We are all created
in the image and likeness of God.[13]

The general definition of the word holy in biblical context is "to
be dedicated to, or consecrated for the service of God."[14]
Consecrated means, "To be dedicated to a sacred purpose."[15]
Sacred means, "Dedicated or set apart for the service of a
deity."[16] In other words, to be holy means to be set apart. To
live a holy life for God means to live in a way that is separate
from general society, in the purpose and for the service of God.

The purpose of God's instructions to us is not to take all of the
fun out of life, but to give us tools to have a healthy mind, body
and spirit to maximize the potential that God has instilled in us.
The following lesson entitled "12 Steps to Holy Living" will give
us some of the tools we need to begin, or continue on, a

successful journey. If you have a Bible, then turn your attention now to the book of Colossians and read 2:20-3:17. When you are finished reading, skip to page 55. If you do not have a Bible then the scriptures are provided below.

12 Steps to Holy Living
Based on Colossians 2:20-3:17

Text:

Colossians 2:20-23

20   Since you died with Christ to the basic principles of this world, why, as though you still belonged to it, do you submit to its rules:
21   "Do not handle! Do not taste! Do not touch!"?
22   These are all destined to perish with use, because they are based on human commands and teachings.
23   Such regulations indeed have an appearance of wisdom, with their self-imposed worship, their false humility and their harsh treatment of the body, but they lack any value in restraining sensual indulgence.

Comment: Just saying "no" doesn't work (see v. 23)

Question: How, then, do you restrain "sensual indulgence"?

Colossians 3:1-17

Rules for Holy Living
1   Since, then, you have been raised with Christ, set your hearts on things above, where Christ is seated at the right hand of God.
2   Set your minds on things above, not on earthly things.
3   For you died, and your life is now hidden with Christ in God.
4   When Christ, who is your life, appears, then you also will appear with him in glory.

52

5	Put to death, therefore, whatever belongs to your earthly nature: sexual immorality, impurity, lust, evil desires and greed, which is idolatry.
6	Because of these, the wrath of God is coming.
7	You used to walk in these ways, in the life you once lived.
8	But now you must rid yourselves of all such things as these: anger, rage, malice, slander, and filthy language from your lips.
9	Do not lie to each other, since you have taken off your old self with its practices
10	and have put on the new self, which is being renewed in knowledge in the image of its Creator.
11	Here there is no Greek or Jew, circumcised or uncircumcised, barbarian, Scythian, slave or free, but Christ is all, and is in all.
12	Therefore, as God's chosen people, holy and dearly loved, clothe yourselves with compassion, kindness, humility, gentleness and patience.
13	Bear with each other and forgive whatever grievances you may have against one another. Forgive as the Lord forgave you.
14	And over all these virtues put on love, which binds them all together in perfect unity.
15	Let the peace of Christ rule in your hearts, since as members of one body you were called to peace. And be thankful.
16	Let the word of Christ dwell in you richly as you teach and admonish one another with all wisdom, and as you sing psalms, hymns and spiritual songs with gratitude in your hearts to God.
17	And whatever you do, whether in word or deed, do it all in the name of the Lord Jesus, giving thanks to God the Father through him.

Inside the above verses, we find the 12 Steps to Holy Living. Below is a breakdown of each step:

Step 1   <u>Put to death, therefore, whatever belongs to your earthly nature</u>: sexual immorality, impurity, lust, evil desires and greed, which is idolatry. Because of these, the wrath of God is coming. (v.5-6)

One piece of advice that I give to everyone who is trying to change relates to this step. My advice is, whenever your flesh feels like doing something, force yourself to do the opposite. There is nothing wrong with pleasure, but many times our feeling and desires can get the best of us.

We naturally desire foods and snacks that are bad for us. We have a natural desire to always want more of things because our flesh is never satisfied. We have a natural desire to idolize people and things. Admiration is one thing, making idols is another.

The way that we put these desires to death is to starve them. In other words begin to practice disciplines that will feed our spirit. Disciplines like eating healthy foods when we feel like snacking. Or, when we get the impulse to buy more or acquire more, we tell ourselves that we don't need it and begin to thank God for what we already have. This is how we do the opposite of what our flesh would desire for us to do.

Step 2   But now <u>you must rid yourselves of all such things</u> as these: anger, rage, malice, slander, and filthy language from your lips. (v.8)

The next thing we must do is learn to control our actions and our language. This is another area where we must do the opposite of what our flesh wants to do. There are times when occurrences take place and we become angry. When this happens, our natural desire is for vengeance. We want to repay evil with evil and at the minimum speak things that are evil.

This is a theme that our society teaches us at all levels. How many times have we seen a movie where a person has been wronged at the hands of another? This victim is usually being violated in some way by a person who is more powerful, and has more resources. Throughout the story we see the victim begin to strategize ways that he or she can overtake the perpetrator. In the end, when the vic-tim becomes the vic-tor we all cheer.

Now, there is nothing wrong with standing up for ourselves and fighting evil. However, when we begin to exercise rage, slander and filthy language, then we are not reflecting the God that we serve. In other words, when our natural desire for vengeance against evil transforms us into evil people, then we are no longer living for God, but for ourselves.

Step 3   Do not lie to each other, since you have taken off your old self with its practices (v.9)

I have had the opportunity to work with children and youth for the majority of my life. I have children of my own, and I remember being a child myself. Through the years I have come to one conclusion…we are born liars!

Even from childhood, we will lie under various circumstances. Without any formal training or observing others, we exercise the evil art form of lying. Whether we feel like we are going to get in trouble, or whether we feel like we will be rewarded we all have a natural propensity to lie. In fact, in our society we have learned to differentiate big lies from small lies. Most people will accept certain lies, as long as they're not harmful to others.

The practice of lying can turn into a habit, and is a mark against Godly character. Lying is not only an action that is against God, but it fosters distrust between people. This is a practice that contradicts living a Godly life and hinders healthy relationships.

Steps 1 through 3 focused on what we are not to do, steps 4 through 12 advise us of what we should do.

Step 4   Therefore, as God's chosen people, holy and dearly loved, <u>clothe yourselves</u> with compassion, kindness, humility, gentleness and patience. (v.12)

There are two implications in this verse. First you have an illustration of one putting clothes on. Second, you have implied message of choice. When most of us wake up in the morning each day, we have a choice of what we will wear. There are even some who have so many clothes, they spend quite some time standing in front of the closet pondering their wardrobe combination for the day.

Likewise, when we wake up in the morning, there are characteristics that we must "put on" before we even get out of the bed. Unfortunately, many have made the excuse of not being able to operate in such characteristics as gentleness and patience using the classic statement, "That's just not who I am." However, we have a choice to "put on" the characteristics that are either in line with God's word, or against God's word.

One helpful exercise in making it easier to put on the "clothing" that would glorify God is to remember all of the times when we behaved horribly, and God had compassion on us and was gentle and patient with us. Remembering that we are not flawless, and many times find ourselves in need of someone's compassion and kindness will help us to clothe ourselves appropriately.

We will find more concepts of remembering and "clothing" ourselves in the next two steps.

Step 5	Bear with each other and forgive whatever grievances you may have against one another. <u>Forgive as the Lord forgave you.</u> (v.13)

If we want to live the life that God has for us, we have to be free. One of the things in life that hinders us the most is our inability to forgive. The process of forgiveness is one of holding and releasing. When we choose not to forgive, we are choosing to hold onto anger, resentment, and memories that keep us from forward progress in our lives. We are choosing to keep others in a state of "indebtedness" by our feelings toward them and how we treat them.

Most importantly, however, when we choose not to forgive we are forgetting all of the times that God forgave us. We forget the broken promises that we made to God and others, yet time and time again, God saw fit to forgive us. As mentioned previously, remembering God's love, compassion, mercy, grace and forgiveness toward us, especially when we were least deserving, will put us in a perfect position to forgive others.

Step 6	And over all these virtues <u>put on love</u>, which binds them all together in perfect unity. (v.14)

Here we see a continuation of step 4 which admonished us to "clothe ourselves" properly. Here the text is informing us of the key element that holds all of the characteristics together. Everything that we do, everything that we say, everything that we believe is bound in love.

The term "bind" gives us the indication that it is love that brings unity to all that we do. In fact, none of these steps can be done properly without our love toward God, and our sincere desire to love others. The fact that love binds these actions together, informs us that these acts are nothing if done separately. If we keep love as our motive, then these things will follow. If I love my brother, then I will not slander him. If I love my sister, then I will forgive her. Love is indeed the tie that binds.

| Step 7 | Let the peace of Christ rule in your hearts, since as members of one body you were called to peace. (v.15a) |

In Session 5, we learned what it meant to be members of the Body of Christ. If we are representatives of Christ, then we must strive for the things that he stood for. If we are going to walk in Christ, then we must walk in peace.

However, according to this text, walking in peace is not enough. We must let the peace of Christ *rule* in our hearts. In other words, peace should sit on the "throne" of our hearts. If love is the tie that binds all things together, then peace is the "king" that governs all things in our lives.

If we are to live as Christians, then peace is the attribute that rules. We are no longer ruled by fear, governed by anxiety, enslaved by anger or driven by the lusts of our passions. We are to allow peace to be the "dictator" under which we live.

If we remember that God has all power, and we recognize that God loves us as his children, then through the power of the Holy Spirit, we can walk in peace. If we allow the peace of Christ to be our ruler, then we will begin to live successfully in God's Kingdom.

| Step 8 | And be thankful. (v.15b) |

In Step 1 we discussed the desires of our "earthly nature." One of our most negative natural qualities is that as human beings we are never satisfied. All of us have the tendency and the temptation to desire more. Whether it is more money, more "toys", a better job, a better home to live in, or a better car to drive, we want more.

But this desire runs deeper. Many of us aren't satisfied with our appearance, our position or our status in life and we do everything that we can to get more. We are obsessed with ambitions that drive us to pursue more status and more stuff, but these same ambitions drive us away from the things that really matter in life.

Now, there is nothing wrong with having drive and ambition and pursuing great things in life. In fact we should maximize the giftedness that God has given us. However, when this drive and ambition is taken over by our natural desire to always have more, then instead of being winners in life, in the end we actually lose.

We lose quality time spent with family and friends. Many times we lose sight of who we are and what we were created to do, while doing things that we don't truly desire just to obtain more stuff and more status. And most importantly, we lose out on quality time and a quality relationship with our Heavenly Father due to lack of focus and misplaced priorities.

What is the solution to being driven by the lust of unhealthy ambition? The answer is simple. Thankfulness! If every time we wanted more we were to stop and take inventory of what we have already been blessed with, our insatiable appetite would be curved. We need to constantly thank God for all that He has already done and all that He has already given us. But most importantly, reflecting on Session 2, we need to be thankful for who God is to us.

Step 9   Let the word of Christ dwell in you richly. (v. 16)

These next two steps are an example of receiving and giving. As you may have noticed, these steps are far easier said than done. If we want to be successful at living out all of these steps, we need constant reminders. These reminders come from the word of Christ which is found in the Bible.

As we will learn in the last session of this book, the Bible is the foundation upon which we stand. It gives us all that we need to be instructed, reminded, encouraged, motivated, corrected and prepared for each day's journey through life. We need to allow this word to dwell, or live in us. The words "richly dwell" give us an illustration of living lavishly. This means that full freedom and possession is being experienced by something.

Many times, if people read the Bible at all, they have a "take some and leave some" approach. They allow some of it into their hearts, and reject some of it. However, what this verse is encouraging us to do is to let the word live lavishly in our lives. Let the word be so in us, that is becomes who we are.

Step 10   ...teach and admonish one another with all
                 wisdom. (v.16)

Continuing from the last step, if the word of God is so in us that it becomes not just what we read, but what we do and who we are, then we will become walking Bibles, if you will. In other words, we will not just be a people who read the word, but we will follow the word. And as we follow the word we will begin to reflect the word, and thus be a reflection of God.

Our next task, then, is to teach the word to others. Now this does not mean that every Christian needs to attend Bible College or Seminary to become the next great theologian. It means that as Christ teaches us, we are to pass that teaching onto others and encourage others through their journey.

Step 11   ...sing psalms, hymns and spiritual songs with
                 gratitude in your hearts to God. (v.16)

Why should we sing? What is the purpose of songs for the Christian? Singing songs to God has a two-fold purpose. One, songs remind us of who God is and all that He has done for us and for this world. Two, they remind us to be thankful at all times and in all circumstances.

Consider the lyrics of this song, "I sing because I'm happy, I sing because I'm free, for His eye is on the sparrow, and I know He watches me."[17] This is an example of gratitude toward God.

Step 12   And whatever you do, whether in word or deed,
            <u>do it all in the name of the Lord Jesus</u>, giving
            thanks to God the Father through him. (v. 17)

So far, we have learned 11 steps for holy living. We have
learned all of the things that we should do to put us on a path that
will lead us to walk in God's direction. This step is our
conclusion. It is the crescendo to this passage.

In everything that we do, our sole purpose and our sole motive is
to glorify God in and through the name of Jesus. This means that
the reason that we do all of these things, is to reflect our Father's
love through the example of Christ, to the entire world.

Knowing this will help us when we feel like our efforts are
fruitless and our lives are meaningless. Knowing this will help us
when people don't see our sacrifice, or recognize our
faithfulness. This will motivate us when no one says "thank
you", and it feels like our detriments outweigh our benefits.

When we do everything for our Father, and walk after the
example of Jesus, God is pleased. When we continuously give
thanks for all things and through all things, our souls will be
pleased.

Questions:

1.   In your opinion, why does God give us "rules" to live by?

_____
_____
_____

2.   According to the above text why doesn't "just saying no"
       work for us?

_____
_____

3.   Which of the 12 Steps do you feel you most need God's
       help?

- _____
- _____
- _____

Conclusion:
There is a reason why there is a 12 Step Program for recovery for
those who struggle with addiction. There is a need for tangible
steps, rather than simple statements and slogans. Likewise, there
is a need for followers of Christ to have tangible steps for living a
Christ-like life. These steps are a great start as we learn to
become doers rather than just hearers.

Having steps to follow is an essential part of our success.
However, *having* the steps is the easiest part. Walking each step
can be extremely difficult. This is why we need help. Each of
the sessions thus far has given us insight into where our help
comes from.

We learned so far that the Holy Spirit is our Counselor, our
helper and our guide. We also learned that prayer is a powerful
element of our connection to God in receiving from Him all that
we need throughout our journey. Further, we learned that as
Christians, we belong to a body of believers who provide a
community of help for us if we only ask.

As you read through these lessons one concept has been, and will
continue to be repeated. This walk of faith was never meant for
us to walk alone. Though we may be able to exist in isolation,
we will not be able to fulfill our purpose, and live out God's
design for our lives without walking with, loving and serving
others.

NOTES/PERSONAL REFLECTION

NOTES/PERSONAL REFLECTION

SESSION 7: HOW DO WE WALK IN OUR CALLING?
Understanding Spiritual Gifts

Introduction:
God has uniquely created us and, with great detail, designed us
for a particular purpose. The word of God tells us in Psalm
139:13-14, *"For you created my inmost being; you knit me
together in my mother's womb. I praise you because I am
fearfully and wonderfully made; your works are wonderful, I
know that full well."* With our unique design we also have
various gifts that God has given us. In this session we will learn
about Spiritual Gifts and how they lead us to our purpose in life.

God-Given Talents vs. Spiritual Gifts:
Though these concepts are often confused, there is a difference
between God-given talents and spiritual gifts. There are some
who are gifted musicians, some who are outstanding athletes, and
others who possess the highest intelligent quotients and brilliant
minds in the world. These are talents. Talents are skills or
abilities that one possesses to perform a particular task.

Spiritual gifts are different than natural skills or abilities. As
reflected in Session 1, all human beings are also spiritual beings.
Therefore, it is not uncommon for all human beings to possess
some form of spiritual giftedness. There are two types of
spiritual gifts:

Type 1:   General Spirituality

✆   Have you ever had a feeling that something was wrong
        without having specific evidence?

✆   Have you ever had a déjà vu experience where you saw
        someone or experienced something that you swear that
        you saw or experienced before?

✆   Have you ever had a dream that amazingly came true?

✆   Have you ever had "psychic" experiences, visions or premonitions that, not only felt real, but actually came true?

These could have been spiritual encounters, and could fall into the generic category of spiritual gifts. Again, as spiritual beings, we have a connection to a spiritual world around us. We cannot simply dismiss spiritual activity because we do not understand it.

There are many instances in the Bible where both followers and non-followers of God had spiritual abilities. Let's look at two examples:

Aaron's Staff

"The LORD said to Moses and Aaron, "When Pharaoh says to you, 'Perform a miracle,' then say to Aaron, 'Take your staff and throw it down before Pharaoh,' and it will become a snake." So Moses and Aaron went to Pharaoh and did just as the LORD commanded. Aaron threw his staff down in front of Pharaoh and his officials, and it became a snake. Pharaoh then summoned <u>wise men and sorcerers</u>, and the <u>Egyptian magicians</u> also did the same things by their secret arts: Each one threw down his staff and it became a snake. But Aaron's staff swallowed up their staffs. Yet Pharaoh's heart became hard and he would not listen to them, just as the LORD had said."
Exodus 7:8-13

Simon the Sorcerer

"Now for some time a man named Simon had practiced sorcery in the city and amazed all the people of Samaria. He boasted that he was someone great, and all the people, both high and low, gave him their attention and exclaimed, 'This man is the divine power known as the Great Power.' They followed him because he had amazed them for a long time with his magic. But when they

believed Philip as he preached the good news of the kingdom of God and the name of Jesus Christ, they were baptized, both men and women. Simon himself believed and was baptized. And he followed Philip everywhere, astonished by the great signs and miracles he saw.

When the apostles in Jerusalem heard that Samaria had accepted the word of God, they sent Peter and John to them. When they arrived, they prayed for them that they might receive the Holy Spirit, because the Holy Spirit had not yet come upon any of them; they had simply been baptized into the name of the Lord Jesus. Then Peter and John placed their hands on them, and they received the Holy Spirit.

When Simon saw that the Spirit was given at the laying on of the apostles' hands, he offered them money and said, 'Give me also this ability so that everyone on whom I lay my hands may receive the Holy Spirit.'

Peter answered: 'May your money perish with you, because you thought you could buy the gift of God with money!'"
Acts 8:9-20

These examples illustrate people's ability to perform magic, sorcery and other miracles. There are more examples in scripture of other "spiritual" giftings as well. However, there is another category of spiritual gifts.

Type 2:   Gifts of the Holy Spirit (Spiritual Gifts from God)

This category pertains to abilities given to us by God through the Holy Spirit. This is the category that the Bible refers to when the phrase "Spiritual Gifts" is used in the New Testament.

What is the purpose of Spiritual Gifts?

"Now to each one the manifestation of the Spirit is given for the common good"   1Corinthians 12:7

Spiritual Gifts are given through the Holy Spirit to all who accept Jesus Christ to equip and strengthen one another, to draw all people to Christ and to bring glory to God.

How can you tell the difference between a Type 1 gift of general spirituality and a Type 2 gift of the Holy Spirit?

In general, you can tell the difference by asking the question, "Is this gift bringing glory to God?" Is the action taken glorifying God, giving insight or clarity into the word of God, or drawing someone closer to God? There are times where this answer may not be so clear, however, the truth will reveal itself.

What are some specific examples of Spiritual Gifts?

"To one there is given through the Spirit the message of wisdom, to another the message of knowledge by means of the same Spirit, to another faith by the same Spirit, to another gifts of healing by that one Spirit, to another miraculous powers, to another prophecy, to another distinguishing between spirits, to another speaking in different kinds of tongues, and to still another the interpretation of tongues. All these are the work of one and the same Spirit, and he gives them to each one, just as he determines." 1 Corinthians 12:8-11

According to scripture, here are a few examples of Spiritual Gifts:

∅   The message of wisdom

     Deeper understanding and insight into physical and spiritual ideals and concepts

∅   The message of knowledge

     Knowledge related specifically to Christianity and religious matters

Ø   Faith

A stronger than normal trusting belief and conviction

Ø   Healing

The ability to be used as a healing agent

Ø   Miraculous powers

The ability to perform miracles

Ø   Prophecy

The ability to be used as a conduit for a message of God to an individual or group. This message can be one of present or future, but must be consistent with scripture, and will not be in conflict with what God has already spoken to the person(s) receiving the word of prophecy. In this context, prophecy does not consist of the forecasting of future world events or the addition of scripture, for these have already been addressed in the Bible.

Ø   Distinguishing between spirits

This gift is an answer to the previous question, "How can you tell the difference between a gift of general spirituality and a gift of the Holy Spirit?" There are some who are gifted with the ability to distinguish between gifts and spirits that glorify God, and those that do not.

Ø   Speaking in different kinds of tongues

The word in this text used for tongues also means "languages outside the normal patterns of intelligible speech."[18] There are some who are gifted to speak in what is known as a spiritual language which is incomprehensible without the gift of interpretation. This gift is also used in prayer which is commonly known as a prayer language. There have also been documented cases (including in scripture) where people have been used of God in to speak in different languages that they have not previously learned for the benefit of others.

℘   Interpretation of tongues

Like that of speaking in tongues, or other languages, there are instances where people who bear this gift will have the ability to understand individuals who are speaking in languages that they have not previously learned, and interpret what they are saying to another individual or group who does not understand.

This gift can also be used to interpret proclamations made in a spiritual language, or tongue. Again, the purpose of this gift is to interpret statements that are incomprehensible for the sake of an individual or group.

Do all gifts exist today?

There is nothing in scripture that states that Spiritual Gifts ceased to exist, or that they were only temporary. However, some gifts seem to have been more prevalent in the early church than they are today. We need to be careful, however, of over-sensationalizing gifts of the Spirit to one extreme, or limiting the Spirit to the opposite extreme. We need to be open to the Spirit of God and the power to accomplish the will of God, even when we don't completely understand it. Again, this is where faith comes in.

Does everyone get every gift?

"All these are the work of one and the same Spirit, and he gives them to each one, just as he determines."
                    1 Corinthians 12:11

"Are all apostles? Are all prophets? Are all teachers? Do all work miracles? Do all have gifts of healing? Do all speak in tongues? Do all interpret?"
1 Corinthians 12:29-31

In the first passage, we see that the Holy Spirit gives gifts to each as he determines. In other words, we do not choose which gifts we will have, though we should be open to receiving all of them. In the second passage, the writer is implying that the answer is no. Not all people receive all gifts.

What about the gift of speaking in tongues?

The gift of tongues has been, and will continue to be an area of controversy for the Church. However, if one of the purposes of the Spirit is unity in the Body of Christ, then we need to beware of divisive teaching. Here are some statements that will give us insight into this topic.

1. The gift of speaking and/or interpreting tongues is, indeed, a Spiritual Gift

2. The gift of speaking and/or interpreting tongues is not given to everyone. (Recall 1Corinthians 12:29-31)

3. The gift of speaking in tongues without interpretation does not foster unity

4. The gift of tongues in personal prayer, or in a corporate setting with interpretation is powerful

What is the baptism of the Holy Spirit?

According to Joel 2:28-32, there is an "outpouring" of the Holy Spirit.

In Matthew 3:11, John the Baptist instructs that he would baptize with water, but Jesus would baptize with the Holy Spirit.

71

The word baptize means "to plunge, dip or wash for the purpose of renewing or establishing a relationship with God."[19] Therefore, the baptism of the Holy Spirit is a divine immersion or saturation of the Holy Spirit as given by God.

Some believe that this baptism is received at the moment one accepts Christ. Others believe that this baptism occurs simultaneously with the act of water baptism. Yet others believe that this is an act that is separate from the acceptance of Christ and the act of water baptism.

Interestingly, there are scriptural references for all three theories. What is most important to remember, is that the Holy Spirit moves in many different ways. Thus, to limit the Spirit of God with theories and doctrine will only result in division.

What does it mean to be filled with the Spirit?

In Acts 19 the Apostle Paul is "filled" with the Spirit long after he has already received the Spirit.

In Ephesians 5:18 there is a comparison between being "drunk with wine" and being "filled" with the Holy Spirit. Coupled with the analogy of being "filled" or literally drunk with wine, the meaning of being filled is to be taken over, or to be completely controlled by. In other words, to be filled with the Holy Spirit means to allow the Spirit to completely control you. This allusion also gives the sense of choice indicating that you must choose to surrender control to the Holy Spirit regularly.

Questions:

1.   What do you think is the difference between a talent and a Spiritual Gift?

_____
_____
_____

2.   What is the purpose of Spiritual gifts?

_____
_____
_____

3.   Are there any gifts that you don't believe exist today?

_____
_____
_____

4.   What Spiritual gifts do you have (or think you have)?

• _____
• _____
• _____

Conclusion:
What is at the "Center" of the Gifts?

1 Corinthians 13 is commonly known as the "love chapter." It is no coincidence that Paul teaches on Spiritual gifts in chapters 12 and 14 and places this love chapter in the middle. Thus, it should be noted that at the center or the heart of all spiritual gifts is love. It is love that unifies us. It is love that binds us. It is love that motivates us. It is in love that the Spirit of God is most representative of God because God is love. Power, gifts, signs and wonders are nothing to God if not packaged in, and delivered with love.

"If I speak in the tongues of men and of angels, but have not love, I am only a resounding gong or a clanging cymbal. If I have the gift of prophecy and can fathom all mysteries and all knowledge, and if I have a faith that can move mountains, but have not love, I am nothing. If I give all I possess to the poor and surrender my body to the flames, but have not love, I gain nothing."
1 Corinthians 13:1-3

NOTES/PERSONAL REFLECTION

SESSION 8: WHERE DO WE STAND?
Understanding the Bible

Introduction:

As Christians, one of the many great gifts that we have been given from God is the very word (or words) of God, The Holy Bible. The Bible gives us tools for living, a road map for navigating through life, inspiring words to motivate us, insight into our purpose in life and a foundation upon which to stand. Understanding the Bible and its teachings are key to walking in faith.

Here are some facts about the Bible.

1.   The Bible is not a book but a collection of books.

These books containing "scriptures", or holy writings, have been assembled together to form what we know as The Holy Bible.

2.   Scriptures were inspired by God.

The Protestant Bible contains 66 books written by over 30 authors covering a period of thousands of years penned in various regions of the world. And no book contradicts another. This could only be accomplished through the inspiration of God.

"All Scripture is God-breathed and is useful for teaching, rebuking, correcting and training in righteousness, so that the man of God may be thoroughly equipped for every good work."
                                2 Timothy 3:16-17

The word in scripture used for "inspired" literally means "God-breathed." It means that God had divine influence on every author of every book in the Bible as to create unity in the word of God. It is also interesting to note that though God had influence, the authors' creativity and personal writing styles are very present throughout the scriptures.

Bible Formation

∅   The Bible is divided into two testaments, the Old Testament and the New Testament.

∅   A testament is a covenant or agreement between God and people.

∅   The Old is the covenant between God and Moses. It is known as the covenant of the <u>law</u>.

∅   The New is the covenant of <u>grace</u> through Jesus Christ. This is God's action on behalf of humanity.

∅   The Bible was originally written in Hebrew, Greek and Aramaic languages.

∅   In the original texts there were no chapters, verses or punctuations.

Who decided which books would be in the Bible?

A council of Christian scholars decided the standard for determining the inspired books of the Christian Bible. Because of this standard, these books of the Bible are referred to as the Canon (literally standard or rule).

Various Christian traditions are not in full agreement as to which books should comprise the Scripture but at minimum, all agree that the 66 books of the Protestant Bible are authoritative and canonical.

Basic Structure:

The basic Bible format presents the Old Testament first, followed by the New Testament.

The Old Testament:

- ☒ Written mostly in Hebrew with a few short passages in Aramaic

- ☒ Was translated in to Greek which is called the Septuagint

- ☒ Most Bibles written in English are translations from these languages

- ☒ The translation used by the Roman Catholic Church is a Latin translation which is known as the Vulgate

Structure of the Old Testament:

- ☒ There are 39 books in the Old Testament

    5   Books of law

    12   Books of history

    5   Books of poetry

    5   Books of Major Prophets

    12   Books of Minor Prophets

Structure of the New Testament:

🗡   There are 27 books in the New Testament

     4   Gospels of Jesus Christ

     1   History

     1   Prophecy

     21   Epistles or letters

What books are "missing" from the Protestant Bible?

The books that are not included in the Canon are referred to as the Apocrypha, which means "obscure or hidden".[20]

Facts about the Apocryphal Books:

🗡   The Apocrypha books were written mostly in Greek with some Hebrew

🗡   The Jewish Church considered them uninspired

🗡   The Jewish Church, at times, refers to them for history

🗡   Never quoted by Jesus

🗡   Early Churches permitted them to be read for edification, but rejected them from the Canon

🗡   Authorship of most books is unknown

🗡   Roman Catholic Church recognizes many of the books

🗡   Some Bible translations will include these books

What are the books of the Apocrypha?

I and II Esdras
Tobit
Judith
Additions to Esther
Wisdom of Solomon
Ecclesiasticus
Baruch
Letter to Jerimiah
Bel and the Dragon
I, II, III, and IV Macabees
The Prayer of Manasseh
Prayer of Azariah and the Song of the Three Young Men

If I want to begin reading and studying the Bible, what is the best version?

Remember, as mentioned earlier, the scriptures were originally written in Ancient Hebrew (a language which is no longer in use), Greek and Aramaic. Any Bible that you purchase today is a translation from these original languages.

Many traditional churches prefer the use of the King James Version. The King James Version is an older translation into Old English language. Though the words and phrases are highly memorable and quite poetic, many people today find the language difficult to understand. The language of the King James Version can be compared to the language of the writings of William Shakespeare.

Today, in the English Language, the best word-for-word and phrase-for-phrase translations come from the American Standard Version (ASV) and the Revised Standard Version (RSV) respectively. Though these are good translations, some find that the writing doesn't flow well for the reader.

Today, many people choose the New International Version because of its relation to everyday American English language. Whatever the version you choose, here are three tips for finding a Bible:

- ✍   Choose a version that is a translation (like those mentioned above) and not a paraphrase of a translation

- ✍   Choose a version that consists of language that you can understand

- ✍   Find a Study Bible which includes footnotes, commentaries, maps, and other helpful tools in one book

Questions:

1.   What does the word "Bible" mean?

_____
_____
_____

2.   What do you believe is the purpose of the Bible?

_____
_____
_____

3.   What can you do to become more familiar with the Bible?

- _____
- _____
- _____

Conclusion:

The Bible is God's written revelation of Himself to mankind. Due to modern technology and scholarship, translations of the Bible exist in most languages around the world. For those who are unable to read, the Bible exists on tape, compact disc and DVD. For those who cannot see or hear, the Bible exists in Braille.

Can one receive Christ and live a Christian life without having or reading the Bible? The answer is yes. However, access to the word of God can help us to live a life of power and confidence in Christ. It can give us daily tools to navigate through life. It can give us hope through situations that seem hopeless. It can increase our faith when our faith is waning. It can guide us to our purpose in life, teach us how to serve those in need, and motivate us to have an impact on humanity to the glory of God. This Book of books is our spiritual foundation upon which we stand.

The Bible is the key to help us in:

✠ Understanding our Spiritual Journey - What we are looking for

✠ Understanding God – Who we are looking for

✠ Understanding Salvation - Which is being offered

✠ Understanding Prayer - How we make the connection

✠ Understanding The Church - Who walks with us

✠ Understanding our Walk – Where and how we go

✠ Understanding Spiritual Gifts – How we walk in our calling

✠ Understanding the Bible – Where we stand

NOTES/PERSONAL REFLECTION

_____

_____

_____

_____

_____

_____

_____

_____

_____

_____

_____

_____

_____

_____

_____

_____

NOTES/PERSONAL REFLECTION

NOTES/PERSONAL REFLECTION

ABOUT THE AUTHOR

E. Dwayne Cantrell is currently the Pastor of Ministry Development at Pasadena Church in Pasadena, CA. He earned a Master of Arts Degree in Education from San Jose State University in San Jose, CA, and a Master of Arts Degree in Theology from Fuller Theological Seminary in Pasadena, California. Dwayne also serves as an administrator at a Christian college preparatory high school, in Pasadena, CA. He and his wife Angel are the founders of Unlimited Impact ministries (www.unlimitedimpact.org) and have two children, a son, Jared, and a daughter, Jada.

To contact the author:

E. Dwayne Cantrell
dwayne@yescorp.org

To order copies of this book:

Go to www.unlimitedimpact.org

or contact the publisher at

www.wipfandstock.com

Endnotes

[1]   Quotations from Think Exist.com

[2]   Quotations from Think Exist.com

[3]   Paraphrase of Frederick C. Mish, John M. Morse, et al. eds., Merriam-Webster's Collegiate Dictionary, Tenth Edition (Springfield: Merriam-Webster, Incorporated, 1999), 49.

[4]   Mish, 75.

[5]   Frederick William Danker, Greek-English Lexicon of the New Testament and Other Early Christian Literature, (Chicago and London: The University of Chicago Press, 2000), 766.

[6]   Danker, 50.

[7]   Tommy Walker, He Knows My Name, (Elkton, MD: Doulos Publishing, 1996).

[8]   Danker, 303.

[9]   Danker, 303.

[10]   Mish, 633.

[11]   Mish, 633.

[12]   Danker, 679.

[13]   Genesis 1:27

[14]   Danker, 10.

[15]   Mish, 245.

[16]   Mish, 1029.

[17]   Words by C. D. Martin, Located in The New National Baptist Hymnal, 21st Edition, (Triad Publications, 1977 revised 2001), 60.

[18]   Danker, 201.

[19]   Danker, 164.

[20]   Mish, 54.

www.ingramcontent.com/pod-product-compliance
Lightning Source LLC
Chambersburg PA
CBHW071107090426
42737CB00013B/2525